N

in the C

Herbert O'Driscoll

Anglican Book Centre
Toronto, Canada

1995
Anglican Book Centre
600 Jarvis Street
Toronto, Ontario
M4Y 2J6

Copyright © Herbert O'Driscoll

All rights reserved. No part of this book may be reproduced, stored in a retrieval system, or transmitted, in any form or by any means, electronic, mechanical, photocopying, recording, or otherwise, without the *written permission* of the publisher.

Canadian Cataloguing in Publication Data

O'Driscoll, Herbert, 1928–
   Marriage : in the Christian church

(Pastoral series)
ISBN 1-55126-132-4

1. Marriage – Religious aspects – Christianity.
I. Title.   II. Series: O'Driscoll, Herbert,   1928–
Pastoral series.

BV835.037 1995   248.8'44   C95-932130-6

*Let their love for each other
be a seal upon their hearts,
a mantle about their shoulders,
and a crown upon their foreheads.*

Book of Alternative Services, page 534

Herbert O'Driscoll has written many popular books on Bible interpretation and Celtic spirituality. A well-known broadcaster and speaker, he has travelled widely throughout North America, Europe, and the Holy Land. In this series he explains, clearly and simply, what it means to be a Christian, and shows how Christianity enriches our everyday living.

Books in this series include

Birth: Holding Your Newborn Child
Baptism: Saying Yes to Being a Christian
Marriage: In the Christian Church
Eucharist: The Feast that Never Ends
Grace: For a Time of Sickness

About This Book

All sorts of people come to the church requesting marriage. They may already be involved in the life of the church. They may know a great deal about it and be familiar with its language and its worship. They may have been involved in the church at one time but have left it. They could be coming to the church for the very first time, without the foggiest notion of what this strange place is about. They may know only that their partner wants to have this marriage service in a church; so they have agreed to go along. Quite often both partners arrive at the church with hopes of being accepted for marriage, but without knowing why they wish this. They may have only a vague feeling that it is something special and somehow significant.

Wherever you and your partner are in all this, these pages are for you. You won't find any jargon in this booklet. You may even be surprised by how little 'religion' seems to be in it. In fact, there is a great deal of religious thinking in these short pages, but it comes to you in the language of life and of everyday experience.

The purpose of this book is to help you realize what it means to be married in a Christian church. It will show you the church's expectations and hopes for your life together. When both you and your partner have read this, the church hopes that you will want to return and discuss the possibility of your marriage further.

Does the church have a hidden motive in giving you this book? Of course it does! If you are already a Christian by upbringing, the church hopes that Christian faith will become clearer and more attractive to you. If you have never been Christian, the church hopes that one day you will find the Christian community attractive enough and exciting enough to join it. In this way, you will come to encounter the person without whom there would be neither Christian faith or church—Jesus Christ.

The choice is yours. Whatever you decide, the church wishes you joy and blessing in your life together.

Herbert O'Driscoll

Most of the titles of these short pieces are taken from the service called *The Celebration and Blessing of a Marriage.* This service can be found on page 528 of one of the Church's prayer books called *The Book of Alternative Services.* There is also a service called *The Form of Solemnization of Matrimony* which can be found on page 563 of *The Book of Common Prayer.* Copies of both of these books can be found in most Anglican churches.

You've made a decision

So it looks as if this is it. You are about to get married. Whether it has been an easy or difficult decision, it is certainly one of the most important you will ever make.

Maybe Christian faith is, at present, part of your lives. Maybe it used to be, but things changed. Maybe it is just about to become part of your lives again. Time will tell. For now, one thing we do know is that the two of you have decided to come to the Christian church to express the mysterious new reality you have discovered—each other. You have decided that this discovery is so deep and real that you want to spend the rest of your lives together.

The church will express this new reality in your lives by offering you the ancient and lovely words of the marriage service. Some of the words we will say, and the deceptively simple actions we will do, on your wedding day link you with men and women far back in time and all over the world. This is important. It tells you that your marriage is much more than an event in your own lives. It is linked with the whole vast web of human life and society.

Society is made up of such human links. If your

marriage is strong and lasting, then it will feed a kind of strength and resilience into the whole human enterprise. Later on we will come across a stage in the marriage service where this is expressed.

But now you are here, hoping to be married in the Christian church. These few pages are written to make sure that, by the time you stand before the altar, you will be quite clear about the meaning of the things you are asked to say. Sometimes you will be surprised at the depth of meaning in these words. There is a reason for this depth. It is because the basic pattern and content of this service has been around for a very long time. It has 'learned' a great deal about human nature. After all, people have been coming to the church for a long time to be married. It would be strange if the church had not learned a thing or two about human life and love. These few pages are a way of sharing some of these insights with you. Welcome, and enjoy.

In heart, body, and mind

Sometimes gentle language can disguise a very strong and uncompromising position. It is not difficult to see how these opening sentences of the marriage service offer a view of sexuality that differs from much of society's thinking. This view not only differs from but also challenges society's thinking on this.

Take the common expression 'to have sex.' 'When did you last have sex?' is the kind of question we now take for granted on television, in movies, or in books. Notice how neatly sex is isolated and made into a thing, an object, even a product you can 'get' and 'have.' Incidentally, consider how invasive a question this is in a society that otherwise hedges the individual around with endless 'rights,' rights that prevent us asking questions about other very important things, such as a person's faith.

However, back to the subject of sex. The marriage service does not deny for a moment that sex can be one of the most wonderful of human experiences. You have only to read the service to see this. We speak of 'knowing each other with delight and tenderness in acts of love.' That certainly is not short changing sex! Even to read that line is what these days we call a 'turn on.'

But notice how this whole paragraph in the service surrounds sex with something bigger and deeper. It tells us that even though we are sexual beings, we are also more. We are a complex and mysterious blending of heart, body, and mind. Because of this, our sexual relating to one another is never as simple as merely having sex. Deep down we know this without anyone having to tell us. We may indeed have sex with someone, but we always know that something more has happened. It's not just that something has happened *to* us, but that something has happened *between* us.

The marriage service is telling us something. Sex is terrific. It is even more terrific in a loving, lasting relationship.

Husband and wife give themselves to each other

Three times in the first few minutes of the marriage service you will hear something about giving oneself. The first time you will be told that 'husband and wife give themselves to each other.' Then a few moments later, you will both be asked to say 'I will' to a question that asks if you are prepared to 'give yourself' to your partner.

To realize the depth of what is being said in these short exchanges, we need to do a little experiment. We need to say the words with a certain emphasis. In each case we need to come down heavily on the syllable *selves* in 'themselves' and *self* in 'yourself.' When we do this, we realize that the marriage service is trying to get us to understand a most important truth. If this relationship is to work, we need to give our whole and deepest selves to it.

But, we might want to say, that's easy. Our whole and deepest selves are already given to this. Why make such a big deal out of this phrase about giving oneself?

The reality is that it can become a big deal. Giving oneself can be much more difficult for some people than for others. A lot will depend on our upbringing. A lot will depend on how life has been for us so far. Major hurts can make it difficult for us to risk giving ourselves to another person.

Sometimes we find it easier to give things than to give of our own selves. Very often we will give our partner gifts, sometimes extremely expensive things, when what he or she really wants is our time or attention or affection, or even just our listening ear. What we long for in someone we love is his or her deepest self. We can sometimes do the same with children, giving them things instead of giving them something of our own selves.

The degree to which each of you can give yourself to the other will affect your relationship at every level—spiritually, socially, sexually. Giving each other time, listening to each other—really listening—simply being together, sometimes in absolute silence. All of these and many others are ways of giving your self to the other.

Will you honour him/her?

Somehow the word *honour* seems to be less a part of our everyday vocabulary than it used to be. Am I just imagining this? I don't think so. If it is true, it might be a sign of the decreasing role that the idea of honour seems to have in modern life.

Whether or not this is true, there is something about the word *honour* that makes us avoid it. It seems to sound too stilted or too affected to speak of someone's honour. Perhaps it brings to mind images of long-ago duels at sunrise with pistols at twenty paces!

Yet the word *honour* is used four times in the marriage service. In the early part of the service, each of you is asked if you will honour the other. Each of you replies, 'I will.' Later on, as each gives the other a ring, you will say, 'I honour you in the name of God.'

What are you promising to do when you say that you will honour your partner? Perhaps the best way of getting at this is to see what you are promising *not* to do. You are promising that you will never try to use the other person as an object for your own wishes. You will not try to use them in ways that go against their wishes. You will always give your partner the honour of being another human being in his or her own right.

There are many ways of dishonouring a person. Ignoring their wishes and hopes. Insisting that they meet your expectations. Forcing them to respond to your wishes. Demanding that they co-operate with your long-range plans. All of these—and many more—are ways in which you can fail to honour your partner. They can enter the relationship in subtle and gradual ways. Be on the alert for them.

Notice that you promise to honour one another 'in the name of God.' This is significant because in the Christian tradition, as in Jewish tradition, the fact that God is the creator of all means that each one of us is a unique part of that creation. We honour each other as unique creations of God—every one of us is of infinite worth. Makes you want to look in a new way at that person you are going to marry, doesn't it?

Will you protect him/her?

This has echoes of knights in shining armour and distressed damsels, don't you think? There is even the possibility of dragons, because the words imply the existence of certain things from which each of you may need protecting.

In this phrase, with one stroke, the marriage service actually demolishes any imaginary scenarios we might have had involving knights in armour and distressed damsels. It does this in a very subtle way that is easy to miss. It simply asks both of you if you will promise to protect the other. It thereby suggests that, in addition to the distressed damsel and rescuing knight scenario, there may be times when our knight gets into distress and needs some rescuing by a valiant damsel!

All of this has been said lightly, almost tongue-in-cheek, but it refers to a moment in the service when something very serious and important is being said. Each of you promises to protect the other. Gone is the idea of the 'weaker sex,' with its assumption that men are invariably stronger than women. In its place, the marriage service tells us the simple reality.

Both of you have strengths, and both of you have weaknesses. Both of you are given the former to deal with the latter. But, as well, both of you from now on will have each other. Each of you has a different pattern of strengths and weaknesses, so hopefully one of you can produce the resources needed when the other has needs.

Those dragons. Where are they? The simple answer is, everywhere! Some of them are easy to miss because they are inside yourself. Small ones, such as angers, jealousies, the scars of past hurts—that sort of thing. And big ones, such as depression or a sense of failure. Sometimes each of you may need the other to protect you from these and other aspects of yourselves. So—will you protect him/her? If you want protection yourself, you would be wise to!

Will you be faithful?

It sounds so simple. You hardly hear the question because you are so eager to give the answer, 'I will.' And you most certainly mean it. Here beside you is the one person in the world you love more than anyone else, the focus of all your hopes and dreams and desires. Of course you will be faithful! How would it be possible to think otherwise for a single moment?

The reality is that human beings are infinitely complex and subtle. The very qualities you have found attractive in each other are also present in other people. Not quite in the same way, of course. The mixture will always be a little different—the face, the voice, the context of the meeting—but those mysterious things that form relationships can be met again and again. So maybe we should ask again, 'Will you be faithful?'

Something else is true in life. You will both grow, mature, change, develop. Something you do not seek or respond to now may become part of your make-up later on, something you may come to see and long for in someone else. Will you be faithful?

Certainly you can be faithful to one another. In spite of all those tabloid headlines, most people are. But it depends on your both realizing that being faithful doesn't just happen. In the kind of open, free-wheeling society we live in, it can take care and self-discipline. Very often, particularly in the workplace, relationships can develop for all sorts of reasons that make perfect sense. You may find yourself working as a team with someone, helping one another survive pressure, sharing a coffee or a lunch from time to time, planning strategies on the job. The list is endless. All of a sudden you may wake up to the fact that someone is getting very fond of another someone!

Yet another factor is learning to recognize when you and someone else are beginning to play supposedly harmless sexual games. This is called flirting, and it can be great fun. But it can sometimes be fatal to a marriage. So—will you be faithful?

Do you, members of the families of N. and N. give your blessing to this marriage?

A poet named John Donne once said that no one is an island. It's perfectly true. For a while, in recent decades, we tried to deny the truth of this. We spoke of 'doing your own thing.' But none of us lives entirely alone. We may have those who care for us and love us. We may have people to whom and for whom we feel some responsibility. This is true no matter what the configuration may be of the group we call 'family.'

We often make jokes about our families, and very often the joke disguises real feelings. We will sometimes say, 'It's our marriage, not the marriage of our families.' But it cannot help being, in some sense, the marriage of your families. Even if for some sad reason there were no family members present, a marriage service is still linking two families, if only because each of you is a product of your family history.

Whether you wish to or not, both of you bring innumerable traits, habits, assumptions, attitudes, traditions, quirks, hurts, joys, and memories to your new relationship. The first time you joined hands, a whole succession of generations joined hands, back through time.

That's why at this moment—just when you are about to make your mutual vows—this question is asked. It puts into words what is already a reality—the involvement of your families in your past, present, and future. Even if your families are on the other side of the planet, they affect your relationship for good or ill. Your families are within you. In all sorts of subtle ways, the generations of the past look out through your eyes and speak in your voices.

Maybe saying these things will help to show how important a question this is, and how important is the reply, 'We do,' from your families. Remember John Donne's saying that no one is an island. This is never more true than on your wedding day.

Will you do all in your power to support and uphold this marriage?

A human being is an extraordinary mixture of strengths and weaknesses. So is a relationship between human beings. This is what makes us such fascinating and complex creatures. It is also, of course, what can make us extremely frustrating and maddening creatures! It is what makes our relationships fascinating yet frustrating, strong yet fragile, resilient yet sensitive.

All of this is particularly true of a marriage, because it is the most intimate of human relationships. People have wisely observed that the wonder is not that so many marriages fail, but that so many succeed.

There are a lot of pressures on a marriage, particularly in these times. The list of pressures is long, and we don't need to go into all of it here. We do need to mention one aspect of modern life, especially modern city life, that adds to the pressures on a marriage. We are talking about loneliness.

That may seem strange. Loneliness in city life? Isn't the very opposite true? Yes and no. We can have many acquaintances, people we bump into, go for a drink with, meet at a party, pass in the condo block. But that does not necessarily mean we have friends.

Life can be lonely if you don't set out to form relationships with other friends and other couples. Even beyond these friendships, you need to develop at least one or two intimate relationships in which you can share what is going on in your marriage, if such a need develops.

And so this question is asked in the marriage service. It is saying to everyone at your service that life is more than hordes of isolated individuals or isolated families. Beyond the self, beyond even your relationship, there has to be a trusted one, a trusted pair, a trusted group. There has to be some element of community support. This question is really saying to the people present around you that they are far more than spectators on this your wedding day. They are friends, and a part of real friendship is to be around when you are needed.

To have and to hold

These words are very old. They are also lovely and lyrical. They have a rhythm that makes them pleasant to say. If you know any of the psalms in the Bible or in the Prayer Book, these words will remind you of the way in which those long-ago poets would often say things in two slightly different ways. The Twenty-Third Psalm says that the Lord 'leads me ... and feeds me.' 'To have and to hold' has that same echoing quality.

But it has a lot more. Having someone and holding someone are two different things. A marriage can get into difficulty when one partner assumes that he or she 'has' the other, if by 'having' they mean that they no longer need to 'hold' the other.

Having is the end of a process. Holding is an on-going process. We never really 'have' another human being, in the sense that we possess them. We most certainly never really 'have' another person if we mean that we can take either them or their love for granted. We need always, in some sense, to 'hold' the other.

'Holding' the other person does not mean constantly and unremittingly hanging on to them in some insecure way. It does not mean mistrusting the other. Good, healthy 'holding' means doing in the marriage what you did before it. It can mean paying attention to the other, knowing what pleases him or her, sensing moods, intuiting when talking or silence is right for a particular moment. It can mean actually saying the words *I love you*. It can also mean 'holding' the other in your heart, constantly having his or her well-being in mind, thinking about and caring for him or her when you are apart. It may sometimes involve a simple and natural prayer for this other human being who has come to mean so much to you.

To do such things is to send a strong and clear message. Such things say, 'I know that in a deep sense I have your love as you have mine, but I want to hold on to you and to your love, as I hope you want to hold on to my love.' We may never actually say these words, but this is the message that will be communicated.

For better, for worse

Have you ever noticed that whenever people say this phrase, they almost always get it wrong? Quite often, when a married couple are trying to work something out and the resolution isn't easy, one of them will make a good-natured joke to lighten the atmosphere. One of them will say to their spouse, 'Well, we did say that this was for better or worse, and I guess this is a bit of the worse!'

Notice the mistake? It's a small one but a very important one. People almost always recall their marriage vow as saying 'for better or worse.' But that is not what the marriage service says. The service asks us to say to each other, 'I take you to be my wedded wife/husband for better, for worse.'

The difference in the language is tiny. It's even smaller than a word. Literally it is only the difference of a single letter, *for* instead of *or*. But what a huge difference in meaning!

When we promise something 'for better, for worse,' we are acknowledging one of the great realities of life. We are acknowledging that we don't have a choice. Without doubt, there will be both better times and worse times in the days and years ahead. There will be joys and sorrows, healings and hurts, surprises and disappointments, successes and failures, satisfactions and frustrations. Life is always a both/and rather than an either/or affair. Life offers no deals, as in 'for better or worse.' In a culture that loves the idea of choice, that wants all of life to be full of choices, this marriage service has some news! Some things do not offer us a choice!

The promise 'for better, for worse' is a promise that you will meet both aspects of life together, enjoying and celebrating the 'better,' facing and taking on the 'worse.' Mysteriously, if we do this, we find that even the worst of the 'worse' can become a lot better.

For richer, for poorer

Just as people tend to misquote 'for better, for worse' when they recall their marriage vow, so also do they tend to misquote this part of their vow. We don't say 'for richer or poorer'—as we usually tend to recall it. Instead we are asked to promise that we will take the other as our spouse 'for richer, for poorer.'

Again, the first and most important thing to notice about what we have said is that it does not give us a choice. It is important to realize this, because we live in a culture that is convinced that life is all about choices. 'Surely there is some way out of this,' we will say in some circumstances of life. Usually we mean something like, 'Is there some easy way out of this that isn't too costly?' Sometimes there is not, because real life, as distinct from life as we wish it to be, is like that.

So here we are, about to opt into a relationship in full knowledge that there will be 'richer' times and 'poorer' times. But the words *richer* and *poorer* refer to more than finances.

It is quite possible that your future may be 'richer' all the way, both in financial terms and in terms of your relationship. Some people who have been married for six or seven decades will tell you honestly that it grew richer and richer the whole way along, and they would not exchange a day of it for anything else. Sometimes that is because they were incredibly lucky. Luck is a part of life. But it may also be because the quality of their relationship worked on whatever happened and made it 'richer.'

One certainty is that both of you bring 'richer' and 'poorer' parts of your selves to this relationship. Each of you is richer in some elements of your personality and poorer in others. It is essential to realize that you marry the poorer or weaker parts of your partner, even though—and here is where romantic love can play some of its tricks—you fell in love with your partner because of what you saw as his or her richer or stronger attributes!

For the rest of our lives

Six deceptively small words. This service is full of such words—small, seemingly harmless, but full of huge implications. These words of the marriage service are like those infinitely tiny silicone chips that can be piled by the score on the end of a finger, yet contain the entire Encyclopedia Britannica in one chip. These are some small words!

Look at this set of six. The short statement they make has a vast meaning. It sits here innocently on the page of the service, waiting for you both to come to it after you have said a number of other things. The progression of the marriage vow is rather like the series of tests or challenges people move through in stories of romantic quest. The biggest test is kept until the end. That's when the fiercest opponent has to be faced, the most fiery dragon. This may seem a strange way to talk about one of life's happiest moments, but even the quest for happiness includes challenges. In fact, attaining some happiness in life depends to a large degree on how we face challenges.

You both promise to have and to hold, to love and to cherish. Then comes the big statement—'for the rest of our lives.'

We need to be clear about something here. These six words collide head on with much in our culture. They challenge all those glib articles in glossy magazines that airily dismiss the possibility—sometimes even the desirability—of marrying for life. You can't have it both ways. If you marry at a Christian altar, you make a promise for life. The church is absolutely up front about this. If you find this impossible in the years to come, the church will certainly not rejoice. It will try to understand, and it will not condemn you. You see, the church has been around for a long time, a lot longer than glossy magazines and breezy lifestyle columnists. It knows something they don't know, although some of them may learn it as they grow older—that a wonderful lifelong relationship is perfectly possible. If you look around, you may come across someone who has had one. Ask them.

With all that I am and all that I have...

Many people will say after a wedding, 'What a beautiful service'—and they will be quite right. Your wedding will be beautiful. So it should be, as it celebrates one of the most significant moments in your life. But if we are really prepared to hear what the words of the service are saying to us, we may find ourselves discovering more than its beauty. We may find ourselves discovering something very different, suddenly hearing our own surprised voices saying such things as 'What a tough service' or 'What a demanding service.'

Look at this particular statement you say to each other as you give a ring. It would be easy to hear this statement merely as a nicely balanced piece of poetry, saying much the same thing twice, each time in a slightly different way. But we would be very wrong.

Who we are and what we have are two very different aspects of ourselves. I may have limitless possessions, but that says very little, if anything, about who I really am. Admittedly, I may become very well known if I have a large number of possessions. This does not always follow but, on the whole, it's true. Many people will know of me if I develop a very high public profile. But even then the public profile of me may be very different from the reality of who I am and what I am like to live with.

The marriage service is not talking about who you are in this sense. This statement is trying to get at something much more important than having other people know you in a public way. In this moment of the marriage service, you are probing deep down to the person you really know yourself to be. At that depth you are offering yourself to the other person.

There is something more implied in this promise. Not only are you offering this other person all that you are at this moment, but you are also offering them all that you are capable of becoming, all that is potential in you.

Once again there is a subtle irony at work here. As you listen to your partner giving you this total gift of his or her self, always remember that, in accepting it totally, you accept both the good and the bad! You see, being a human being always involves some small print in the agreements we make with each other!

Almighty God, look graciously upon the world that you have made ... and especially on all whom you make one flesh in holy marriage.

At first sight, it may seem strange to link something so personal as your particular marriage with the concept of the whole world! Why do so at this stage in the service?

This is not the only time Christian faith links something that seems purely personal with the whole world. When the Virgin Mary, the mother of our Lord Jesus Christ, was informed that she would bear a child, she sang a song. We call it the Magnificat because her first sentence was, 'My soul magnifies the Lord.' It's a strange and wonderful song. Mary expresses her deeply personal joy and her hopes for the child, but she also expresses what most people would think of as very revolutionary thoughts about the whole of human society.

Mary sees that her child will somehow affect the whole world. In a sense, your marriage will affect the whole of humanity. This may make you want to smile in disbelief, for surely this is sheer exaggeration. Far from it! The truth is that your marriage, this encounter of your two lives, your intention to forge them together into a new unity called your marriage—this is bringing into being a new reality. The moment it happens, it enters into and becomes part of the vast tapestry of human life and human affairs. It will begin a chain of cause and effect that will continue to the end of time, in ways utterly beyond our knowing.

Think of the vast compliment Christian faith pays to you both. In society in general you are regarded in various ways, none of them overly thrilling—as a taxpayer, a social insurance number, even as that coldest of designations in our culture, a consumer. Not so in the context of Christian faith. By regarding you as an integral part of the whole human story, the church gives significance and meaning—even a kind of glory—to your lives, your love, and your marriage.

May N. and N. so live together that the strength of their love may enrich our common life.

Perhaps the best way to uncover the meaning of this prayer for your future relationship is to mention something about wedding photographs. In every wedding album there is at least one photograph where the bride and groom are facing each other and gazing into each other's eyes.

So it should be. There is nothing wrong with such a stance, and it would be strange if it were otherwise. But there is another photograph one never sees in the album. If it were included, it would look rather strange, and it could easily be misunderstood. So nobody takes it. Yet if we did, we would be expressing the interest and hope of this prayer for your relationship. The missing photograph would show the two of you together, perhaps holding hands, yet facing away from each other, looking out towards the world around you.

By imagining this photograph we are trying to uncover the meaning of this prayer being offered for your lives. This prayer asks that you may come to realize you have both received a gift, the gift of your mutual love. You have received this together, and at the same time, each of you has received the gift of the other. But these gifts have been given to you for a purpose beyond themselves and beyond yourselves. They are given to you so that you may return something to the society in which you live. As the prayer expresses it, the hope for you both is that your love will enrich not only both of you, but also the society you live in and the lives of people you come into contact with in various ways.

Why bring this in at such a most personal moment as your wedding? Because Christian faith believes that life is lived individually, but in the context of society. Life is both personal and communal, private and public, possessed and shared. Christian faith says even more. It believes that when we share our lives for the common good, we are doing what our Lord did in sharing his divine love and life by coming into the life of our world. That's the reason for this prayer for you.

May they receive the gift and heritage of children and the grace to bring them up to know and to love you.

It's amazing the number of people who arrive at marriage plans without ever discussing children. Of all the things to be discussed, this is the big one! Ironically, many people who feel ultra-modern because they have no problem discussing sex can entirely ignore the subject of children, a possibility not entirely unconnected with their sex life!

The church wants you to be aware of four simple, but all-important, things. The first is that a child is by far the most significant heritage you can give to the future. The two of you may fully intend to be millionaires before you're thirty, but whether you reach that goal or not, your ultimate riches will be the quality of your children's lives.

The second thing you need to know is that even in an age when you may feel you can plan your family to the *n*th degree, the birth of a child to you is as much the gift of God as it ever was.

That's the part about having children. In some ways—only some—that may be the easier part. After this, there is a lifetime of work ahead of you, if you are prepared to take it on. This is not the place to list all that this entails, but it is the moment to mention the third thing the church wants you to realize. Whether you are rich or poor financially, the most precious thing you can give your child is Christian faith. Why? Because if you do this, you give him or her a solid base for meaning and direction. You give them a kind of lens through which they can make some sense of reality. All the CD-Roms and videos in the world can't give your child a faith. Virtual Reality will always fall a long way short of the ultimate reality called God.

The fourth thing is about your child loving God. There is no formula to make that happen. But there is one thing we have learned over thousands of years—the best way to make it happen is to have your children learn, from your love for them and your love for each other, how much the love of God means to you both.

May those who have witnessed these vows find their lives strengthened and their loyal ties confirmed.

On your wedding day, you will be facing away from your family and friends for most of the service. This means that you will be partially in a world of your own. To some extent, this is as it should be, but you need to know that a lot will be going on behind you.

You would be able to see some of it if you turned around. Some people are smiling. A few here and there are a bit teary. Some people are whispering. But that is only the surface of things. The real agenda is, for the most part, unseen. Not only do you two not see it; neither does anyone else, with the possible exception of some very sensitive people who intuit what is going on.

Like all human events, marriage services are more than merely personal. There is a universal level to what is primarily your day. What is a totally new experience for you is a memory of a long-ago wedding day for someone behind you. For someone else, seeing you two standing side by side is a reminder of someone they once stood beside who is no longer with them, either through the pain of divorce or the agony of bereavement. Someone else will be regretting a marriage that just didn't work out. Someone else will be looking forward to their own marriage. For another couple behind you, this ceremony may be the clincher that makes them decide to go ahead and plan marriage for themselves.

Here and there in the congregation behind you, there will be some wise and sensitive couples who are making your marriage vow a silent remaking of their own. They may not be saying anything. They may touch each other in some way, who knows. But when you two go down the aisle on your way out, you will not have been the only couple to have said Yes to each other in that service. Others will have piggy-backed on your joy and your love to say Yes again to each other.

If you're wise, the two of you will do that more than once in the years ahead.

Let their love for each other be a seal upon their hearts, a mantle about their shoulders, and a crown upon their foreheads.

At various times in your service there could be music, or you may have arranged for something to be sung. Whether or not this is so, there will be moments when the language of the service itself will sing to you. This is such a moment.

These words come in the middle of a prayer that is said just after you have been married. It's a long prayer, and it would be understandable if on your wedding day your mind wandered. However, you would be wise to listen carefully, because the prayer is a kind of song—a very beautiful song—sung for both of you.

The images are vivid and lovely. We are asking that, for you, love may be a seal, a mantle, and a crown. As we ask these things for you, we are travelling a long way back in time and over many miles. You are hearing the echoes of ancient traditions, coming back into Western life after having been lost for centuries.

When we seal something, we are sending a signal that, whatever it may be, it is extremely important and valuable and it is to remain so for a long time into the future. This is our prayer for your marriage. The image of the mantle comes from Jewish life. A shawl or mantle goes on one's shoulders for prayer. An echo of this is the stole that the priest will wear while celebrating your marriage service. The prayer asks that the two of you may be bound together by a single mantle, and that you will know that you are always in the presence of God.

The image of the crown comes from Orthodox Christian tradition. For a moment in the marriage service, a small crown is placed on the heads of both bride and groom. For that moment they are 'royal,' the unique beings God created us to be. This prayer is telling you that your real worth—what makes you of priceless value as a human being—is the presence of the divine life within you.

In marriage is represented the spiritual unity between Christ and his Church.

At first sight, you would be excused for wondering what this has to do with your getting married. If you did wonder, it would be quite understandable. We will look and see why this statement comes at this point in your marriage.

The best way to start is by noting something we know to be a fact. If Jesus of Nazareth had not been born, there would be no such thing as the Christian church. One could, of course, argue that someone else would have come into the world and formed something like it, but then the result would have turned out to be very different.

Christians believe that it is the events that took place in the last few days of our Lord's life that made all the difference. We call these events his crucifixion and his resurrection. These are the events that brought into being a faithful community, which then began to form and express and pass on the Christian faith.

The crucial thing is this. It took Jesus' willingness to sacrifice himself to bring this Christian community into being. This is where the relationship between you and your partner comes in. A marriage, at least a good marriage, can be healthy only when both partners are ready to do some 'dying.'

What does that mean? Some self-centredness has to die, some self-will, some personal freedoms. To say they must die sounds negative. But not really. The church is not asking you to become less than you are. In its long wisdom, the church is pointing you to a great truth. If each of you is prepared to do some sacrificing of the self—which is what our Lord did totally—then mysteriously, something new comes into being. From his sacrifice, the Christian community came into being. From your willingness to sacrifice elements of your selves comes the birth of a new reality, a strong vibrant marriage where individual desires and hopes give place to the desires and hopes of both together, the married couple.

A decision to be made

At some stage in your discussions with the person who is going to conduct your wedding service, you may find yourselves talking about whether or not there will be Holy Communion, or a Celebration of the Holy Eucharist, in the service.

This will depend on a number of things. First, it will depend on whether or not either of you has been baptized into the Christian faith. It could also depend on whether either or both of you have been, in any regular way, part of a worshipping Christian community in recent years. There may be other reasons why this has to be decided carefully. There may be a difference of tradition in your two families. This may affect your decision.

If you do decide to share the Holy Eucharist, you will find that it adds a whole new dimension to your marriage service. For instance, one of the things you will be able to do at a certain point in the ceremony is to bring the bread and the wine and water to the altar for the sacrament. In fact, your very first action together after making your marriage vows will be to bring those gifts to God. This can become a metaphor for your lives. Time takes you on a lifetime journey into God, to whom you both offer your gifts of mind, body, and spirit. As the two of you receive the consecrated bread and wine, you are linked together by receiving the body and blood of Jesus.

In the kind of world we live in, you are going to need every possible resource to have a strong, lasting, joyful relationship. The church offers you resources that have stood the test of centuries. In this sacred meal, the church offers you access to a love even stronger than your love for each other. It offers you the eternal love of God for you both.

Think this one over carefully. Listen to good advice. If in the end you decide to include this sacred Christian meal, have a look at the pages that follow. Come to think of it, why not look at them anyway? Who knows what changes to your thinking and your life the future may bring? If not now, perhaps some day this simple receiving of sacred bread and wine may become something of immense significance to you.

The Lord's table

Christian faith can sometimes be very down to earth. What is a table doing in your marriage plans? Well, to start with, you will probably have a number of them at your reception. But there are at least three other tables you should be aware of. One is present in an ancient story or vision, one is here in the church, and one will be in your home. Since the one in church is often called an altar, you may not realize that it too is a table.

Christian faith inherited the idea of a central table from Judaism, our Lord's own tradition. Judaism says that if you want to imagine ultimate shalom—peace and unity and reconciliation— you should imagine a great table set at the heart of the universe. Everyone is welcome at it. Everyone has more than enough to eat and drink. Everyone at this table is equal. Judaism honours this dream or vision by gathering families around the Passover table in the home.

Christians honour this vision by remembering that the night before Jesus died, he gathered his disciples around a table in an upper room. That is why you will stand in front of a table, or altar, on your wedding day.

That is two of the tables we mentioned. The

third is—or soon will be—in your home. Hopefully some day you will have children at your table. You will find that there is something about eating together that is more than just eating together. Relationships seem to grow richer and deeper around a table. Sometimes problems can be dealt with over a meal. Sometimes intimate things can be brought up between the two of you. If and when you have children, you will find that the family table is often the place where questions can be asked and—only sometimes!—answered. Jokes can be shared and, often silently, love can be communicated. Sometimes you can suddenly realize with a very pleasant shock that the table at home has in a wonderful and mysterious way become the Lord's table!

So what has all this to do with Christian faith? Everything. You would be amazed at how many disguises God can wear in order to be present among you at the family table, even in your arguments. Even in those bad jokes!

*We remember his death,
we proclaim his resurrection,
we await his coming in glory.*

By now you will have moved through the actual marriage service. You will be just about to share the sacred bread and wine. This is the symbolic meal that Jesus gave us. He told us to share this meal until the end of time. At a certain moment we will all say these words together. What do they mean?

Obviously they mean something about our Lord. We are saying three things—that he died, that he rose from the dead (and goes on doing that), and that Christians look for his return.

We are trying to express some very mysterious ideas. To say this is not a cop-out. Both of you have already encountered very mysterious stuff when trying to communicate your love for each other. What we are trying to express here is the heart of what Christians believe about Jesus. We believe that he lived a life of utter obedience to God. We believe that something in our humanity rejected that and finally killed him. We believe that somehow he was fully present among his followers after his death. We also believe that because he is a living reality for untold millions of people twenty centuries later, Jesus continues to be present among us. Finally, we believe that this mysterious capacity to move beyond death to new life is the mystery at the heart of all creation. This will turn out to be the last truth to be discovered when God completes the whole of creation.

This is mind-boggling stuff. It's far bigger than anything the script writers of *Star Trek: The Next Generation* ever dreamed up. What's more, if we continue the television reference for a moment, this 'series' called Christian Faith has been on the air now for about two thousand 'seasons,' and the planetary audience is getting larger, not smaller! Any 'program' that lasts that long must have something going for it! In this case, it might just be because it is—as Jesus himself said—the way, the truth, and the life.

Bring us to that city of light where you dwell with all your sons and daughters.

Once again you may feel like asking what this has to do with your marriage. A great deal, but we need to unwrap the language a bit to find this out.

At the heart of Christian faith there is a dream or vision. It's the same kind of dream that Martin Luther King Jr had when he said 'I have a dream.' His dream was of a society where peace and justice and harmony reigned. In a sense, this is also the dream of Christian faith. It is not surprising that the visions are alike, because King was a very great Christian.

The Christian dream is the dream of Jesus. He called the dream or vision the kingdom of God. It's a vision of all creation as it would be if the will of God ruled, if the will of God was always done. John, one of Jesus' followers, wrote a book in the Bible called Revelation. In the book, John imagines the perfect state of things as a city. It is full of light, peace, beauty, justice, and, incidentally, is in total harmony with nature.

You might ask what use such a dream has in our world, which is so far from that wonderfully perfect state. The answer is that here on earth the Christian vision has inspired countless men and women to work towards such things as peace and justice and harmony, in the structures of their society and time. Somehow the heavenly dream has turned out to be immensely energizing here on earth!

This is the dream the Christian church offers you when we celebrate the Eucharist at your wedding. It is more than an offer. It is really an invitation. The church is asking you to dream this dream in your own lives, to try to find out what Jesus meant when he envisioned this kingdom of God. You and I are invited to work and to live in such a way that we become builders of that kingdom, using our own dreams and gifts and energy and love. Try it for a while, and see how much sense it makes of life in general.

Go in peace to love and serve the Lord.

The service is just about to end. The organist's hands will be poised over the keys. Some people will be groping for camera range-finders. Just at this moment, the church dismisses you.

That may sound strange. In our culture, to dismiss someone means that you are brushing them aside. Not so with the church and the two of you. If you remember that the word *dismiss* is really from a Latin word meaning 'to send out,' you begin to get the picture. That is exactly why it is used just as you are preparing to turn and go down the aisle together. You are not being dismissed. You are being 'sent out.' There is a lot of difference.

The church is doing even more. It is sending you out 'in peace.' There is a beautiful Hebrew word from which the English word *peace* comes. We have used it from time to time—the word *shalom*. It means a great deal more than the English word *peace*. If the church says *shalom* to you on your wedding day, it is wishing the two of you a deep unity in your relationship. It is also praying that somehow life may all come together for you, that you may be at peace within yourselves, at peace with each other, at peace with the world around you, at peace with God. You can see that an awful lot is packed into that old Hebrew word *shalom*.

Then the church says one last thing to you. It doesn't say it in so many words right here. It is something that the church has been saying to you throughout this service. It says that your best hope of finding satisfaction and meaning in life will depend on what you decide life is about. Is it about loving and serving yourself or about loving and serving something or someone greater and higher than yourself?

If you decide on the latter, then the church offers you someone that you can both serve and love, even while you serve and love each other. Loving and serving this person doesn't mean that life must become a twenty-four-hour-a-day religious trip! You can serve and love this person by being who you are, doing what you do, using your gifts and your energies and the best of who and what you are. That someone is the person we have referred to many times in talking about your marriage service. His name is Jesus Christ.